We are Gross,
But We Help!

I0439578

Early Reader
Children's Picture Books

Written By B. Keith Davidson
Illustrated By Kissel Cablayda

JD-Biz Publishing

We are Gross, But We Help!

My name is Molly Millipede,
I'm a Detritivore.

MILLIPEDE?

Maybe you've never heard of us,
But you've seen us before.

Many people think we are scary,
that we look really weird.
They chase us with swatters and sprays,
they think we should be feared.

Detritivores are animals,
we clean up Nature's mess.

And when it comes to recycling,
you know we are the best!

All animals and plants leave waste,
they drop it on the ground.

If there were no detritivores,
you could not walk around.

Now you're in for a special treat,
but do not be afraid.

Today we are joining in a,
detritivore parade!

As a millipede I eat leaves,
that lay dead all around.

And I break them down as I chew,
making food for the ground.

The dung beetles and wood lice too,
eat from the forest floor.

I should not tell you what they eat,
but they always want more.

The house fly likes to clean a lot,
he just loves rotten junk.

He would eat garbage all day long,
old hotdogs or cheese hunk.

WE MAY BE STRANGE OR WEIRD TO YOU,

WE ARE GROSS, BUT WE HELP!

My insect friends all get inline,
and they all start to yelp,
"We may be strange or weird to you,
we are gross, but we help!"

But we are not just on the land,
we swim all through the seas.

There's dead stuff in the water too,
we clean it up with ease.

The fiddler crab uses his claw,
to dig up the ground.
Then he sifts dirt in through his mouth,
to see what can be found.

WE MAY LOOK LIKE ALIENS,
WE ARE GROSS, BUT WE HELP!

The fiddler crab walking sideways.
He joins in and starts to yelp,
"We may look like an aliens,
we are gross, but we help!"

Land and water then what comes next,
well that would be the sky.
If you look up you just might see,
detritivores flying by.

Up in the sky, a vulture soars,
its dead things that he seeks.

But people are afraid of the,
bald heads and crooked beaks.

PLEASE DO NOT BE AFRAID OF US,
WE ARE GROSS, BUT WE HELP!

A vulture flies into our midst,
and we all start to yelp,
"Please do not be afraid of us,
we are gross, but we help!"

Not all of us can walk around,
mushrooms for example.

They help breakdown rot every day,
their abilities are ample.

The earthworm is a squiggly guy,
he burrows through the dirt.

IT'S OKAY,
IT DOESN'T HURT

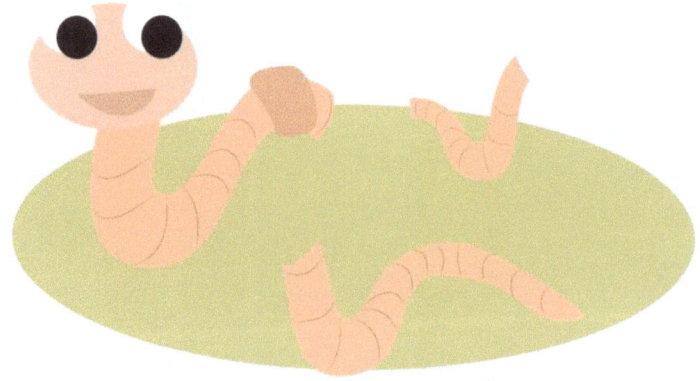

You can cut him into pieces,
he's small, but hard to hurt.

THOUGH WE MAY BE ODD SHAPED
FUNGUS WE ARE GROSS,
BUT WE HELP!

They can't walk so we'll carry them,
they can support our yelp,
"Though we may be odd shaped fungus,
we are gross, but we help!"

Our parade could walk down Main Street,
maybe in your home town.

EVERYONE JUST
CALM DOWN.

There's no reason to get upset,
everyone just calm down.

Detritivores are important,
for the Earth and your health.
If you don't want us around,
you have to clean it yourself!

WE ARE GROSS,
BUT WE HELP!

So next time that you see us out,
please do not scream or yelp!
Remember we are creatures too,
we are gross, but we help!

Author's Bio

B. Keith Davidson is a children's author who lives with his wife and 3 wonderful kids in Windsor, ON. He is a former clown and children's entertainer. His goal with every book is to make someone smile. Even if it is just himself.

Illustrator Bio

Kissel Cablayda is a full time graphic artist and painter based in Davao City, Philippines. When she was 9, she won from a school editorial cartooning contest and from that day on she knew her world will revolve in arts and design. Eleven years later, she graduated with a degree in Bachelor of Arts in Communication Arts Major in Media Arts from the University of the Philippines Mindanao.

Her first and second job was terrible. So she decided to have a home based job and find her passion. Now she happily works as an online book illustrator at Mendon Cottage Books.

She believes that creativity is a journey, not a destination, and that design is an essential part of every human communication and experience. She also believes that unicorns are real.

When she is not designing, she spends her time travelling, watching TV series, reading a bunch of books and cleaning her room. She likes novels written by Chaim Potok, Sidney Sheldon and Harper Lee. She loves Filipino meat cuisine and hates vegetables.

She aspires to excel in her career and make other people's lives be less hard through art and design.

To know more about her, email her at
kisselcablayda2013@gmail.com

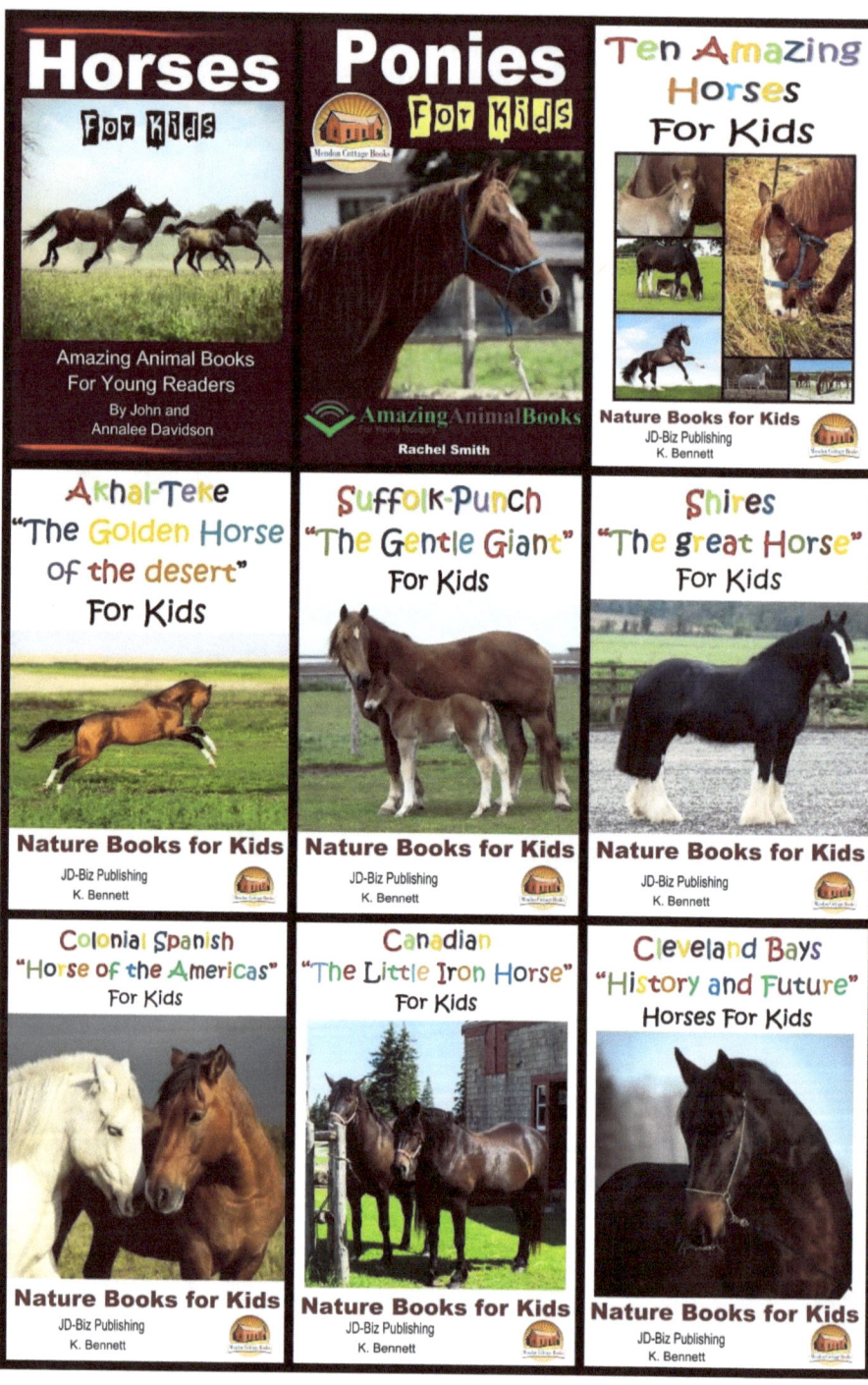

Our books are available at

1. Amazon.com

2. Barnes and Noble

3. Itunes

4. Kobo

5. Smashwords

6. Google Play Books

Download Free Books!
http://MendonCottageBooks.com

Publisher

JD-Biz Corp

P O Box 374

Mendon, Utah 84325

http://www.jd-biz.com/

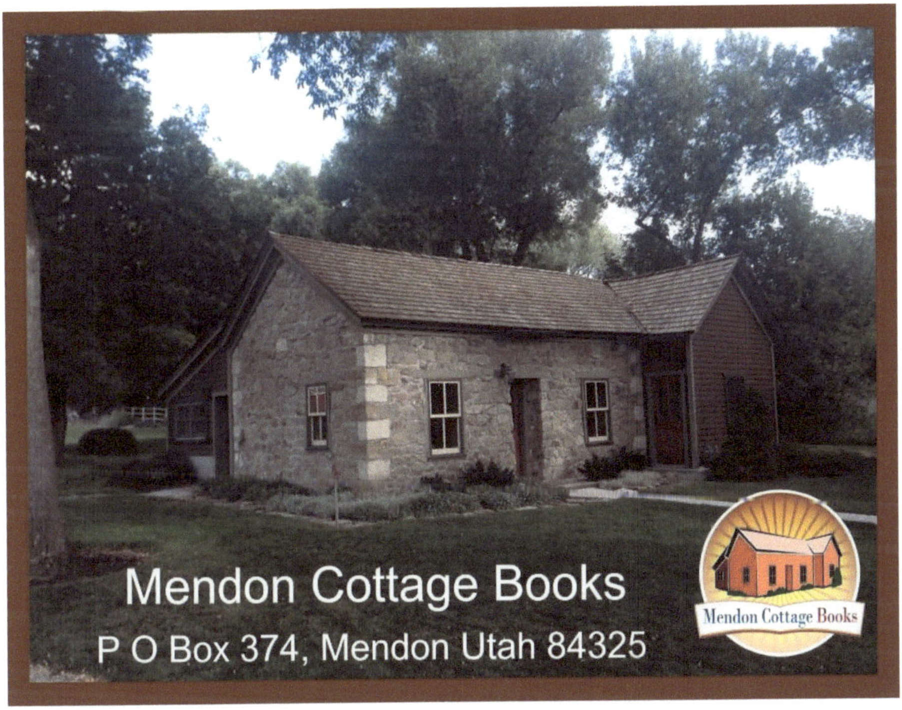